TO

_____

FROM

_____

FAMILY
CHRISTIAN
PRESS

THE REAL SERIES

MAKING
REAL GOOD
FRIENDS

30 DEVOTIONS

The quoted ideas expressed in this book (but not scripture verses) are not, in all cases, exact quotations, as some have been edited for clarity and brevity. In all cases, the author has attempted to maintain the speaker's original intent. In some cases, quoted material for this book was obtained from secondary sources, primarily print media. While every effort was made to ensure the accuracy of these sources, the accuracy cannot be guaranteed. For additions, deletions, corrections or clarifications in future editions of this text, please write FAMILY CHRISTIAN PRESS.

Scripture quotations are taken from:

The Holy Bible, King James Version

The Holy Bible, New International Version (NIV) Copyright © 1973, 1978, 1984, by International Bible Society. Used by permission of Zondervan Publishing House. All rights reserved.

The New American Standard Bible®, (NASB) Copyright © 1960, 1962, 1963, 1968, 1971, 1972, 1973, 1975, 1977, 1995 by The Lockman Foundation. Used by permission.

The Holy Bible, New King James Version (NKJV) Copyright © 1982 by Thomas Nelson, Inc. Used by permission.

The Holy Bible, New Living Translation, (NLT) Copyright © 1996. Used by permission of Tyndale House Publishers, Inc., Wheaton, Illinois 60189. All rights reserved.

New Century Version®. (NCV) Copyright © 1987, 1988, 1991 by Word Publishing, a division of Thomas Nelson, Inc. All rights reserved. Used by permission.

The Message (MSG) This edition issued by contractual arrangement with NavPress, a division of The Navigators, U.S.A. Originally published by NavPress in English as THE MESSAGE: The Bible in Contemporary Language copyright 2002-2003 by Eugene Peterson. All rights reserved.

The Holman Christian Standard Bible™ (HCSB) Copyright © 1999, 2000, 2001 by Holman Bible Publishers. Used by permission.

Cover Design by Kim Russell / Wahoo Designs
Page Layout by Bart Dawson

ISBN 1-58334-336-9

Printed in the United States of America

MAKING REAL GOOD FRIENDS

30 DEVOTIONS

Table of Contents

Introduction

Throughout the Bible, we are reminded to love one another, to care for one another, and to treat one another as we wish to be treated. In other words, we are reminded to be good Christians, and we are reminded to be good friends.

This collection of devotional readings is a celebration of Christian friendship. As such, it is intended to help you be a good friend to others and to choose good friends for yourself.

Perhaps you received this book as a gift from a girl friend or guy friend. Or maybe you just picked it up on your own. Either way, you should take the ideas on the pages seriously.

This text contains 30 devotional readings, one for each day of the month. The ideas in each chapter are powerful reminders of God's commandments—and of the importance of choosing friends who encourage you to be obedient and faithful.

So here's your assignment: Today and every day, resolve to be a trustworthy, encouraging, loyal friend. And, while you're at it, treasure the people in your life who are loyal friends to you. Friendship is, after all, a glorious gift, praised by God. Give thanks for that gift and make it grow.

CHAPTER 1

Pleasing God First

You shall have no other gods before Me.
Exodus 20:3 NKJV

Are you a people-pleaser or a God-pleaser? Hopefully, you're far more concerned with pleasing God than you are with pleasing your friends. But face facts: even if you're a devoted Christian, you're still going to feel the urge to impress your friends and acquaintances—and sometimes that urge will be strong.

Peer pressure can be good or bad, depending upon who your peers are and how they behave. If your friends encourage you to follow God's will and to obey His commandments, then you'll experience positive peer pressure, and that's a good thing. But, if your friends encourage you to do foolish things, then you're facing a different kind of peer pressure . . . and you'd better beware.

To sum it up, here's your choice: you can choose to please God first, or you can fall victim to peer pressure. The choice is yours—and so are the consequences.

The Basics:
What You Need to Know

Your first obligation is to please God, not people.

What the Bible Says

No one has seen God, ever. But if we love one another, God dwells deeply within us, and his love becomes complete in us—perfect love! This is how we know we're living steadily and deeply in him, and he in us: He's given us life from his life, from his very own Spirit.
1 John 4:12-13 MSG

He that loveth not, knoweth not God; for God is love.
1 John 4:8 KJV

Yet, O LORD, you are our Father. We are the clay, you are the potter; we are all the work of your hand.
Isaiah 64:8 NIV

Big Ideas

It takes all time and eternity to know God.

Oswald Chambers

I lived with Indians who made pots out of clay which they used for cooking. Nobody was interested in the pot. Everybody was interested in what was inside. The same clay taken out of the same riverbed, always made in the same design, nothing special about it. Well, I'm a clay pot, and let me not forget it. But, the excellency of the power is of God and not us.

Elisabeth Elliot

A man can no more diminish God's glory by refusing to worship Him than a lunatic can put out the sun by scribbling the word "darkness" on the walls of his cell.

C. S. Lewis

A Prayer for Today

Dear Lord, Your love is eternal and Your laws are everlasting. When I obey Your commandments, I am blessed. Today, I invite You to reign over every corner of my heart. I will have faith in You, Father. I will sense Your presence; I will accept Your love; I will trust Your will; and I will praise You for the Savior of my life: Your Son Jesus.

Amen

CHAPTER 2

Choosing Friends Carefully

Greater love has no one than this,
that he lay down his life for his friends.
John 15:13 NIV

Some friendships help us honor God; these friendships should be nurtured. Other friendships place us in situations where we are tempted to dishonor God by disobeying His commandments; friendships that dishonor God have the potential to do us great harm.

Because we tend to become like our friends, we must choose our friends carefully. Because our friends influence us in ways that are both subtle and powerful, we must ensure that our friendships are pleasing to God. When we spend our days in the presence of godly believers, we are blessed, not only by those friends, but also by our Creator.

Do you seek to live a life that is pleasing to God? If so, you should build friendships that are pleasing to Him. When you do, your Heavenly Father will bless you and your friends with gifts that are simply too numerous to count.

The Basics:
What You Need to Know

Your friends will be a major influence on your life.
So choose your friends carefully.

What the Bible Says

A friend loves you all the time,
and a brother helps in time of trouble.
Proverbs 17:17 NCV

As iron sharpens iron, a friend sharpens a friend.
Proverbs 27:17 NLT

If a fellow believer hurts you, go and tell him—
work it out between the two of you.
If he listens, you've made a friend.
Matthew 18:15 MSG

Big Ideas

Few of the valuable things in life "just happen."
When they happen, it is because we recognize their
importance and devote ourselves to them.
Rule number one for deepening your friendships is this:
Assign top priority to your relationships.

Alan Loy McGinnis

Friends are angels who lift our feet when our
own wings have trouble remembering how to fly.

Anonymous

Do you want to be wise? Choose wise friends.

Charles Swindoll

A Prayer for Today

Thank You Lord, for my friends, the people
who enrich my life. I pray for them today,
and ask Your blessings upon them . . .
and upon me.
Amen

Friends Who Encourage

*So encourage each other and give each other strength,
just as you are doing now.*
1 Thessalonians 5:11 NCV

f you'd like to build a positive life and a positive self-image, hang out with friends who see the world—and you—in a positive light. When you do, you'll discover that good thoughts are contagious, and you can catch them from your friends.

As Christians, we have every reason to be optimistic about life. As John Calvin observed, "There is not one blade of grass, there is no color in this world that is not intended to make us rejoice." But, sometimes, rejoicing may be the last thing on our minds. Sometimes, we fall prey to worry, frustration, anxiety, or sheer exhaustion. And if we're not careful, we'll spread our pessimism to the people we love most. But God's Word instructs us to do otherwise.

In Ephesians, Paul advises, "Do not let any unwholesome talk come out of your mouths, but only what is helpful for building others up according to their needs, that it may benefit those who listen" (4:29 NIV). Paul's words still apply.

Your friends and family members probably need more encouragement and less criticism. The same can be said for you. So be a booster, not a cynic—and find friends who do likewise.

The Basics:
What You Need to Know

You should try to find encouraging friends,
and you should try to be an encouraging friend.

What the Bible Says

*He comes alongside us when we go through
hard times, and before you know it, he brings us
alongside someone else who is going through
hard times so that we can be there for
that person just as God was there for us.*
2 Corinthians 1:4 MSG

*Encourage each other. Live in harmony and peace.
Then the God of love and peace will be with you.*
2 Corinthians 13:11 NLT

*So don't lose a minute in building on what you've
been given, complementing your basic faith with good
character, spiritual understanding, alert discipline,
passionate patience, reverent wonder,
warm friendliness, and generous love,
each dimension fitting into and developing the others.*
2 Peter 1:5-7 MSG

Big Ideas

Do you wonder where you can go for
encouragement and motivation?
Run to Jesus.

Max Lucado

True friends will always lift you higher and challenge
you to walk in a manner pleasing to our Lord.

Lisa Bevere

The truest help we can render an afflicted man
is not to take his burden from him, but to call out
his best energy, that he may be able to
bear the burden himself.

Phillips Brooks

A Prayer for Today

Make me sensitive, O Lord, to the many gifts of
encouragement I receive each day. And, let me be
a source of encouragement to all who cross my path.
The Bible tells of Your servant Barnabas. Like Barnabas,
I, too, want to be an encourager to my family
and friends so that I might do Your work
and share Your love.
Amen

CHAPTER 4

The Right Kind of Peer Pressure

He who walks with wise men will be wise,
but the companion of fools will be destroyed.
Proverbs 13:20 NKJV

ur world is filled with pressures: some good, some bad. The pressures that we feel to follow God's will and to obey His commandments are positive pressures. God places them on our hearts, and He intends that we act in accordance with these feelings. But we also face different pressures, ones that are definitely not from God. When we feel pressured to do things—or even to think thoughts—that lead us away from God, we must beware.

Rick Warren observed, "Those who follow the crowd usually get lost in it." We know these words to be true, but oftentimes we fail to live by them. Instead of trusting God for guidance, we imitate our friends and suffer the consequences. Instead of seeking to please our Father in heaven, we strive to please our peers, with decidedly mixed results. Instead of doing the right thing, we do the "easy" thing or the "popular" thing. And when we do, we pay a high price for our shortsightedness.

Are you satisfied to follow the crowd, or will you follow the One from Galilee? If you sincerely want to please God, you must resist the pressures that society seeks to impose upon you, and you must conform yourself, instead, to God's will, to His path, and to His Son.

The Basics:
What You Need to Know

Your friends should encourage you
to become a better person.

What the Bible Says

Do not be misled:
"Bad company corrupts good character."
1 Corinthians 15:33 NIV

Don't become partners with those who reject God.
How can you make a partnership out of right
and wrong? That's not partnership; that's war.
Is light best friends with dark?
2 Corinthians 6:14 MSG

Friend, don't go along with evil. Model the good.
The person who does good does God's work.
The person who does evil falsifies God,
doesn't know the first thing about God.
3 John 1:11 MSG

Big Ideas

A wise man may look ridiculous in a company of fools.

Thomas Fuller

Those who follow the crowd usually get lost in it.

Rick Warren

You will get untold flak for prioritizing
God's revealed and present will for your life
over man's . . . but, boy, is it worth it.

Beth Moore

A Prayer for Today

Dear Lord, other people may want me to misbehave,
but You want me to behave myself. And that's what
I want, too—I want to do what's right. So help me
do the right thing, Lord, even when it's hard.

Amen

CHAPTER 5

Friends Who Encourage You to Count Your Blessings

In everything give thanks; for this is the will of God in Christ Jesus for you.

1 Thessalonians 5:18 NKJV

Are you basically a thankful guy or girl? Do you appreciate the stuff you've got and the life that you're privileged to live? You most certainly should be thankful. After all, when you stop to think about it, God has given you more blessings than you can count. So the question of the day is this: will you slow down long enough to thank your Heavenly Father . . . or not?

Sometimes, life here on earth can be complicated, demanding, and frustrating. When the demands of life leave you rushing from place to place with scarcely a moment to spare, you may fail to pause and thank your Creator for the countless blessings He has given you. Failing to thank God is understandable . . . but it's wrong.

God's Word makes it clear: a wise heart is a thankful heart. Period. Your Heavenly Father has blessed you beyond measure, and you owe Him everything, including your thanks. God is always listening—are you willing to say thanks? It's up to you, and the next move is yours.

The Basics:
What You Need to Know

You've got more blessings than you can count,
but it doesn't hurt to try

What the Bible Says

*Our prayers for you are always spilling over
into thanksgivings. We can't quit thanking God
our Father and Jesus our Messiah for you!*
Colossians 1:3 MSG

*My counsel for you is simple and straightforward:
Just go ahead with what you've been given.
You received Christ Jesus, the Master; now live him.
You're deeply rooted in him. You're well constructed
upon him. You know your way around the faith.
Now do what you've been taught. School's out;
quit studying the subject and start living it!
And let your living spill over into thanksgiving.*
Colossians 2:6-7 MSG

Big Ideas

The words "thank" and "think" come from
the same root word. If we would think more,
we would thank more.

Warren Wiersbe

The best way to show my gratitude to God is to
accept everything, even my problems, with joy.

Mother Teresa

Why wait until the fourth Thursday in November?
Why wait until the morning of December twenty-fifth?
Thanksgiving to God should be an everyday affair.
The time to be thankful is now!

Jim Gallery

A Prayer for Today

Lord, let me be a thankful Christian.
Your blessings are priceless and eternal.
I praise You, Lord, for Your gifts and,
most of all, for Your Son.
Amen

CHAPTER 6

Keeping God's Golden Rule

Just as you want others to do for you,
do the same for them.
Luke 6:31 HCSB

Life is simply better when we treat other people in the same way we would want to be treated if we were in their shoes. Things go better when we're courteous and compassionate. Graciousness, humility, and kindness are all virtues we should strive for. But sometimes, we fall short. Sometimes, amid the busyness and confusion of everyday life, we may neglect to share a kind word or a kind deed. This oversight hurts others, and it hurts us as well.

Today, slow yourself down and be alert for those who need your smile, your kind words, your hug, or your helping hand. Make kindness a centerpiece of your dealings with others. They will be blessed, and you will be, too. But not necessarily in that order.

The Basics:
What You Need to Know

The Golden Rule is God's rule,
and it should be your rule, too.

What the Bible Says

Let us not become weary in doing good,
for at the proper time we will reap a harvest
if we do not give up.

Galatians 6:9 NIV

Each of you should look not only to your own interests,
but also to the interest of others.

Philippians 2:4 NIV

Carry each other's burdens, and in this way
you will fulfill the law of Christ.

Galatians 6:2 NIV

Big Ideas

Anything done for another is done for oneself.

Pope John Paul II

It is one of the most beautiful compensations of life that no one can sincerely try to help another without helping herself.

Barbara Johnson

We should behave to our friends as we would wish our friends to behave to us.

Aristotle

A Prayer for Today

Dear God, help me remember to treat other people in
the same way that I would want to be treated
if I were in their shoes. The Golden Rule is Your rule,
Father; I'll make it my rule, too.
Amen

CHAPTER 7

Being Patient with Our Friends

Knowing God leads to self-control.
Self-control leads to patient endurance,
and patient endurance leads to godliness.

2 Peter 1:6 NLT

The dictionary defines the word *patience* as "the ability to be calm, tolerant, and understanding." If that describes you, you can skip the rest of this page. But, if you're like most of us, you'd better keep reading.

For most of us, patience is a hard thing to master. Why? Because we have lots of things we want, and we want them NOW (if not sooner). But the Bible tells us that we must learn to wait patiently for the things that God has in store for us.

The next time you find your patience tested to the limit (either by a friend or by events that are happening too slowly for your liking), remember that the world unfolds according to God's timetable, not yours. Sometimes, you must wait patiently, and that's as it should be. After all, think how patient God has been with you!

The Basics:
What You Need to Know

To be a good friend, you need to be a patient friend.

What the Bible Says

*Now we exhort you, brethren, warn those who are
unruly, comfort the fainthearted, uphold the weak,
be patient with all.*
1 Thessalonians 5:14 NKJV

Patience of spirit is better than haughtiness of spirit.
Ecclesiastes 7:8 NASB

*God has chosen you and made you his holy people.
He loves you. So always do these things:
Show mercy to others, be kind, humble,
gentle, and patient.*
Colossians 3:12 NCV

Big Ideas

When I am dealing with an all-powerful, all-knowing God, I, as a mere mortal, must offer my petitions not only with persistence, but also with patience. Someday I'll know why.

Ruth Bell Graham

The next time you're disappointed, don't panic. Don't give up. Just be patient and let God remind you he's still in control.

Max Lucado

It is wise to wait because God gives clear direction only when we are willing to wait.

Charles Stanley

A Prayer for Today

Lord, sometimes I can be a very impatient person.
Slow me down and calm me down. Let me trust in
Your plan, Father; let me trust in Your timetable;
and let me trust in Your love for me.

Amen

CHAPTER 8

Steering Clear of Temptation

No temptation has seized you except what is common to man. And God is faithful; he will not let you be tempted beyond what you can bear. But when you are tempted, he will also provide a way out so that you can stand up under it.

1 Corinthians 10:13 NIV

How hard is it to bump into temptation in this crazy world? Not very hard. The devil, it seems, is out on the street, working 24/7, causing pain and heartache in more ways than ever before. We, as Christians, must remain vigilant. Not only must we resist Satan when he confronts us, but we must also avoid those places where Satan can most easily tempt us. And, if we are to avoid the unending temptations of this world, we must arm ourselves with the Word of God.

In a letter to believers, Peter offers a stern warning: "Your adversary, the devil, prowls around like a roaring lion, seeking someone to devour" (1 Peter 5:8 NASB). What was true in New Testament times is equally true in our own. Satan tempts his prey and then devours them (and it's up to you—and only you—to make sure that you're not one of the ones being devoured!).

As believing Christians, we must beware because temptations are everywhere. Satan is determined to win; we must be equally determined that he does not.

The Basics:
What You Need to Know

Temptation is everywhere.
Find friends who help you avoid it.

What the Bible Says

*Be sober, be vigilant; because your adversary
the devil walks about like a roaring lion,
seeking whom he may devour.*

1 Peter 5:8 NKJV

*The Lord knows how to deliver the godly
out of temptations.*

2 Peter 2:9 NKJV

*Put on the whole armor of God, that you may be able
to stand against the wiles of the devil.*

Ephesians 6:11 NKJV

Big Ideas

We can't stop the Adversary from whispering in
our ears, but we can refuse to listen,
and we can definitely refuse to respond.

Liz Curtis Higgs

Always remember that we can learn to control
our weaknesses through the power of the Holy Spirit
and in doing so become well-balanced individuals
who cannot be controlled by Satan.

Joyce Meyer

Rebuke the Enemy in your own name and he laughs;
command him in the name of Christ and he flees.

John Eldredge

A Prayer for Today

Lord, temptation is everywhere! Help me turn from it
and to run from it! Let me keep Christ in my heart,
and let me put the devil in his place:
far away from me!
Amen

CHAPTER 9

Friendships Built on Trust

Beloved, if God so loved us,
we also ought to love one another.
1 John 4:11 NKJV

All genuine friendships are built upon honesty and trust. Without trust, friends soon drift apart. But with trust, friends can stay friends for a lifetime.

As Christians, we should always try to be trustworthy, encouraging, loyal friends. And, we should be thankful for the people who are loyal friends to us. When we treat other people with honesty and respect, we not only make more friends, but we also keep the friendships we've already made.

Do you want friends you can trust? Then start by being a friend they can trust. That's the way to make your friendships strong, stronger, and strongest!

The Basics:
What You Need to Know

If you want your friendships to last,
then you must be a trustworthy friend.

What the Bible Says

For there is nothing covered, that shall not be revealed; neither hid, that shall not be known. Therefore, whatsoever ye have spoken in darkness shall be heard in the light; and that which ye have spoken in the ear in closets shall be proclaimed upon the housetops.

Luke 12:2-3 KJV

Ye shall not steal, neither deal falsely, neither lie one to another.

Leviticus 19:11 KJV

So put away all falsehood and "tell your neighbor the truth" because we belong to each other.

Ephesians 4:25 NLT

Big Ideas

Two words will help you cope when you run low
on hope: accept and trust.

Charles Swindoll

Sometimes when I was a child my mother or father
would say, "Shut your eyes and hold out your hand."
That was the promise of some lovely surprise. I trusted
them so I shut my eyes instantly and held out my hand.
Whatever they were going to give me I was ready to
take. So it should be in our trust of our Heavenly Father.
Faith is the willingness to receive whatever He wants to
give or the willingness not to have what
He does not want to give.

Elisabeth Elliot

Never be afraid to trust an unknown future
to an all-knowing God.

Corrie ten Boom

A Prayer for Today

Dear Lord, make me a trustworthy friend. Let me
seek the truth and speak the truth. Let me be loyal,
compassionate, and forgiving. And, let Jesus
always be the standard for truth in my life so that
I might be a worthy example to others
and a worthy servant to You.
Amen

CHAPTER 10

Friends Who Aren't Hung Up on Stuff

Do not love the world or the things in the world.
If anyone loves the world,
the love of the Father is not in him.
1 John 2:15 NKJV

Are you a person who's overly concerned with the stuff that money can buy? Hopefully not. On the grand stage of a well-lived life, material possessions should play a rather small role. Of course, we all need the basic necessities of life, but once we meet those needs for ourselves and for our families, the piling up of possessions creates more problems than it solves. Our real riches, of course, are not of this world. We are never really rich until we are rich in spirit.

Our society is in love with money and the things that money can buy. God is not. God cares about people, not possessions, and so must we. We must, to the best of our abilities, love our neighbors as ourselves, and we must, to the best of our abilities, resist the mighty temptation to place possessions ahead of people.

Money, in and of itself, is not evil; worshipping money is. So today, as you prioritize matters of importance in your life, remember that God is almighty, but the dollar is not.

The Basics:
What You Need to Know

Material possessions aren't really that important—
and hopefully material possessions aren't
too important to you and your friends.

What the Bible Says

He who trusts in his riches will fall,
but the righteous will flourish . . . .
Proverbs 11:28 NKJV

For what will it profit a man if he gains the whole world,
and loses his own soul? Or what will a man
give in exchange for his soul?
Mark 8:36-37 NKJV

For where your treasure is,
there your heart will be also.
Luke 12:34 NKJV

Big Ideas

The socially prescribed affluent, middle-class lifestyle has become so normative in our churches that we discern little conflict between it and the Christian lifestyle prescribed in the New Testament.

Tony Campolo

Greed is enslaving. The more you have, the more you want—until eventually avarice consumes you.

Kay Arthur

There is absolutely no evidence that complexity and materialism lead to happiness. On the contrary, there is plenty of evidence that simplicity and spirituality lead to joy, a blessedness that is better than happiness.

Dennis Swanberg

A Prayer for Today

Dear Lord, help me remember that the things in this world that are really valuable are my life, my family, and my relationship with You.

Amen

CHAPTER 11

Beyond the Fear of Rejection

Wherever they do not welcome you, when you leave that town, shake off the dust from your feet as a testimony against them.

Luke 9:5 HCSB

Sometimes, you may feel pressured to compromise yourself, and you may be afraid of what will happen if you firmly say "No." You may be afraid that you'll be rejected. But here's a tip: don't worry too much about rejection, especially when you're rejected for doing the right thing.

Pleasing other people is a good thing . . . up to a point. But you must never allow your "willingness to please" to interfere with your own good judgement or with God's commandments.

Instead of being afraid of rejection, focus on pleasing your Creator first and always. And when it comes to the world and all its inhabitants, don't worry too much about the folks you can't please. Focus, instead, on doing the right thing—and leave the rest up to God.

The Basics:
What You Need to Know

Sometimes it's tough to take rejection . . .
tough but necessary.

What the Bible Says

*If you're not welcomed, not listened to,
quietly withdraw. Don't make a scene.
Shrug your shoulders and be on your way.*
Mark 6:11 MSG

*My dear friends, don't let public opinion influence
how you live out our glorious,
Christ-originated faith.*
James 2:1 MSG

*The fear of human opinion disables;
trusting in God protects you from that.*
Proverbs 29:25 MSG

Big Ideas

When you taste a measure of being able to love and enjoy the people in your life, without having to have any particular response from them, you are tasting bliss.

Paula Rinehart

Every day, I find countless opportunities to decide whether I will obey God and demonstrate my love for Him or try to please myself or the world system. God is waiting for my choices.

Bill Bright

Too many Christians have geared their program to please, to entertain, and to gain favor from this world. We are concerned with how much, instead of how little, like this age we can become.

Billy Graham

A Prayer for Today

Dear Lord, today I will worry less about pleasing other
people and more about pleasing You. I will stand up for
my beliefs, and I will honor You with my thoughts,
my actions, and my prayers. And I will worship You,
Father, with thanksgiving in my heart,
this day and forever.
Amen

CHAPTER 12

Friends Who Help You Celebrate Life

Celebrate God all day, every day.
I mean, revel in him!
Philippians 4:4 MSG

What is the best day for you and your friends to celebrate life? This one! Today and every day should be a time for celebration as you consider God's blessings (starting, of course, with God's ultimate gift: salvation through Jesus Christ).

What do you and your pals expect from the day ahead? Are you expecting God to do wonderful things, or are you living beneath a cloud of worry and doubt?

The familiar words of Psalm 118:24 remind us of a profound yet simple truth: "This is the day the LORD has made; let us rejoice and be glad in it" (HCSB). Our duty, as believers, is to rejoice in God's marvelous creation.

For Christians, every day begins and ends with God and His Son. Christ came to this earth to give us abundant life and eternal salvation. We give thanks to our Maker when we treasure each day. So with no further ado, let the celebration begin!

The Basics:
What You Need to Know

Your life should be a cause for celebration,
and your friends should help you celebrate.

What the Bible Says

David and the whole house of Israel were celebrating with all their might before the LORD, with songs and with harps, lyres, tambourines, sistrums and cymbals.

2 Samuel 6:5 NIV

This is the day which the LORD has made; let us rejoice and be glad in it.

Psalm 118:24 NASB

At the dedication of the wall of Jerusalem, the Levites were sought out from where they lived and were brought to Jerusalem to celebrate joyfully the dedication with songs of thanksgiving and with the music of cymbals, harps and lyres.

Nehemiah 12:27 NIV

Big Ideas

Celebration is possible only through the deep
realization that life and death are never found
completely separate. Celebration can really come
about only where fear and love, joy and sorrow,
tears and smiles can exist together.

Henri Nouwen

I know nothing, except what everyone knows—
if there when God dances, I should dance.

W. H. Auden

If you can forgive the person you were,
accept the person you are, and believe in the person
you will become, you are headed for joy.
So celebrate your life.

Barbara Johnson

A Prayer for Today

Dear Lord, You have given me so many blessings,
and as a way of saying "Thank You," I will celebrate.
I will be a joyful Christian, Lord, quick to smile and
slow to frown. And, I will share my joy with my family,
with my friends, and with my neighbors,
this day and every day.
Amen

CHAPTER 13

Friends Who Make Time for God

He awakens Me morning by morning,
He awakens My ear to hear as the learned.
The LORD God has opened My ear.

Isaiah 50:4-5 NKJV

When it comes to spending time with God, are you a "squeezer" or a "pleaser"? Do you squeeze God into your schedule with a prayer before meals (and maybe, if you've got the time, with a quick visit to church on Sunday)? Or do you please God by talking to Him far more often than that? If you're wise, you'll form the habit of spending time with God every day. When you do, it will change your life.

This book asks that you give your undivided attention to God for at least two minutes each day. And make no mistake about it: the emphasis in the previous sentence should be placed on the words "at least." In truth, you should give God lots more time than a couple of minutes a day, but hey, it's a start.

Even if you're the busiest person on Planet Earth, you can still carve out a little time for God. And when you think about it, isn't that the very least you should do?

The Basics:
What You Need to Know

You should make time each day for God . . .
and your friends should do likewise.

What the Bible Says

*It is good to give thanks to the LORD, to sing praises
to the Most High. It is good to proclaim
your unfailing love in the morning,
your faithfulness in the evening.*

Psalm 92:1-2 NLT

*Truly my soul silently waits for God;
from Him comes my salvation.*

Psalm 62:1 NKJV

*May the words of my mouth and the thoughts
of my heart be pleasing to you, O LORD,
my rock and my redeemer.*

Psalm 19:14 NLT

Big Ideas

If choosing to spend time alone with God is
a real struggle—a heavy-handed demand that
only adds more guilt and stress to your already
overblown schedule—it's time to change
the way you approach his presence.

Doris Greig

I think we Christians have become lazy.
We would rather read a book about how
someone else became closer to God than spend time
alone with him ourselves.

Sheila Walsh

Overcommitment and time pressures are the greatest
destroyers of marriages and families.
It takes time to develop any friendship, whether with
a loved one or with God himself.

James Dobson

A Prayer for Today

Lord, Your Holy Word is a light unto the world;
let me study it, trust it, and share it with all my friends.
Let me discover You, Father, in the quiet moments of
the day. And, in all that I say and do, help me to be
a worthy witness as I share the Good News of
Your perfect Son and Your perfect Word.
Amen

CHAPTER 14

Friends Who Encourage You to Develop Your Talents

*God has given gifts to each of you from his great variety
of spiritual gifts. Manage them well so that
God's generosity can flow through you.*

1 Peter 4:10 NLT

od knew precisely what He was doing when He gave you a unique set of talents and opportunities. And now, God wants you to use those talents for the glory of His kingdom. So here's the big question: will you choose to use those talents, or not?

Your Heavenly Father wants you to be a faithful steward of the gifts He has given you. But you live in a society that may encourage you to do otherwise. You face countless temptations to squander your time, your resources, and your talents. So you must be keenly aware of the inevitable distractions that can waste your time, your energy, and your opportunities.

Every day of your life, you have a choice to make: to nurture your talents or neglect them. When you choose wisely, God rewards your efforts, and He expands your opportunities to serve Him.

God has blessed you with unique opportunities to serve Him, and He has given you every tool that you need to do so. Today, accept this challenge: value the talent that God has given you, nourish it, make it grow, and share it with the world. After all, the best way to say "Thank You" for God's gifts is to use them.

The Basics:
What You Need to Know

You've got talents that you haven't fully developed.
It's time to recognize those talents and develop them.

What the Bible Says

Do not neglect the gift that is in you.
1 Timothy 4:14 HCSB

I remind you to fan into flame the gift of God.
2 Timothy 1:6 NIV

There are different kinds of gifts, but they are all from
the same Spirit. There are different ways to serve
but the same Lord to serve.
1 Corinthians 12:4-5 NCV

Big Ideas

In the great orchestra we call life, you have
an instrument and a song, and you owe it to God
to play them both sublimely.

Max Lucado

God often reveals His direction for our lives
through the way He made us . . .
with a certain personality and unique skills.

Bill Hybels

Not everyone possesses boundless energy or
a conspicuous talent. We are not equally blessed
with great intellect or physical beauty or emotional
strength. But we have all been given
the same ability to be faithful.

Gigi Graham Tchividjian

A Prayer for Today

Lord, thank You for the talents You have given me.
Let me treasure them and use them for Your glory
as I walk in the footsteps of Your Son.
Amen

Friends Who Encourage You to Hope

*But if we look forward to something we don't have yet,
we must wait patiently and confidently.*
Romans 8:25 NLT

ace facts: pessimism and Christianity don't mix. Why? Because Christians have every reason to be optimistic about life here on earth and life eternal. Mrs. Charles E. Cowman advised, "Never yield to gloomy anticipation. Place your hope and confidence in God. He has no record of failure."

Sometimes, despite our trust in God, we may fall into the spiritual traps of worry, frustration, anxiety, or sheer exhaustion, and our hearts become heavy. What's needed is plenty of rest, a large dose of perspective, and God's healing touch, but not necessarily in that order.

Today, make this promise to yourself and keep it: vow to be a hope-filled Christian. Think optimistically about your life, your education, your family, your friends, and your future. Trust your hopes, not your fears. Take time to celebrate God's glorious creation. And then, when you've filled your heart with hope, share your optimism with others. They'll be better for it, and so will you. But not necessarily in that order.

The Basics:
What You Need to Know

Optimistic friends will help you
become a more optimistic person.

What the Bible Says

Make me hear joy and gladness.
Psalm 51:8 NKJV

*My cup runs over. Surely goodness and mercy
shall follow me all the days of my life;
and I will dwell in the house of the LORD forever.*
Psalm 23:5-6 NKJV

I can do everything through him that gives me strength.
Philippians 4:13 NIV

Big Ideas

No Christian can be a pessimist, for Christianity is
a system of radical optimism.

William Ralph Inge

Change your thoughts, and you change your world.

Norman Vincent Peale

We may run, walk, stumble, drive, or fly,
but let us never lose sight of the reason for the journey,
or miss a chance to see a rainbow on the way.

Gloria Gaither

A Prayer for Today

Dear Lord, I will look for the best in other people,
I will expect the best from You, and I will try my best
to do my best—today and every day.
Amen

CHAPTER 16

Friends Who Help You Become a Little Wiser

The Lord says, "I will make you wise and show you where to go. I will guide you and watch over you."

Psalm 32:8 NCV

Are you and your friends wise guys (and girls)? And, are you striving to help each other become a little wiser every day? Hopefully so.

All of us would like to be wise, but not all of us are willing to do the work that is required to become wise. Why? Because wisdom isn't free—it takes time and effort to acquire.

To become wise, we must seek God's wisdom and live according to His Word. To become wise, we must seek wisdom with consistency and purpose. To become wise, we must not only learn the lessons of the Christian life, we must also live by them (and hang out with people who do likewise).

If you sincerely desire to become wise—and if you seek to share your hard-earned wisdom with others—your actions must give credence to your words. The best way to share one's wisdom—perhaps the only way—is not by words, but by example.

Wisdom is like a savings account: If you add to it consistently, then eventually you'll have a great sum. The secret to success is consistency. Do you seek wisdom? Then seek it every day, and seek it in the right place. That place, of course, is, first and foremost, the Word of God.

The Basics:
What You Need to Know

Your friends should help you make wise decisions,
and you should do the same for them.

What the Bible Says

Wisdom is the principal thing; therefore get wisdom.
And in all your getting, get understanding.
Proverbs 4:7 NKJV

Happy is the person who finds wisdom,
the one who gets understanding.
Proverbs 3:13 NCV

Anyone who listens to my teaching and obeys me is
wise, like a person who builds a house on solid rock.
Though the rain comes in torrents and the floodwaters
rise and the winds beat against that house,
it won't collapse, because it is built on rock.
Matthew 7:24-25 NLT

Big Ideas

Wisdom is knowledge applied. Head knowledge is
useless on the battlefield. Knowledge stamped
on the heart makes one wise.

Beth Moore

Knowledge is horizontal.
Wisdom is vertical; it comes down from above.

Billy Graham

Wisdom is the God-given ability to see life
with rare objectivity and to handle life
with rare stability.

Charles Swindoll

A Prayer for Today

Lord, when I trust in the wisdom of the world, I will
sometimes be led astray, but when I trust in Your
wisdom, I build my life on a firm foundation.
Today and every day I will trust Your Word and follow it,
knowing that the ultimate wisdom is Your wisdom
and the ultimate truth is Your truth.
Amen

CHAPTER 17

When People Are Cruel

You have heard it said, "Love your neighbor and hate your enemy." But I tell you: Love your enemies and pray for those who persecute you, that you may be sons of your Father in heaven.

Matthew 5:43-45 NIV

ometimes people can be cruel . . . very cruel. When other people are unkind to you or to your friends, you may be tempted to strike back, either verbally or physically. Don't do it! Instead, remember that God corrects other people's behaviors in His own way, and He doesn't need your help (even if you're totally convinced you're "in the right"). Remember that God has commanded you to forgive others, just as you, too, must sometimes seek forgiveness from others.

So, when other people behave cruelly, foolishly, or impulsively—as they will from time to time—don't start swinging or screaming. Speak up for yourself as politely as you can, and walk away. Next, forgive everybody as quickly as you can. Then, get on with your life, and leave the rest up to God.

The Basics:
What You Need to Know

Sure people can be cruel, but that doesn't mean
that you have to hang out with them.

What the Bible Says

Hatred stirs up trouble, but love forgives all wrongs.
Proverbs 10:12 NCV

Escape quickly from the company of fools;
they're a waste of your time, a waste of your words.
Proverbs 14:7 MSG

Smart people are patient;
they will be honored if they ignore insults.
Proverbs 19:11 NCV

Big Ideas

You can be sure you are abiding in Christ if you are able to have a Christlike love toward the people that irritate you the most.

Vonette Bright

When something robs you of your peace of mind, ask yourself if it is worth the energy you are expending on it. If not, then put it out of your mind in an act of discipline. Every time the thought of "it" returns, refuse it.

Kay Arthur

We are all fallen creatures and all very hard to live with.

C. S. Lewis

A Prayer for Today

Dear Lord, sometimes people behave badly.
When other people upset me, help me to calm
myself down, and help me forgive them
as quickly as I can.
Amen

CHAPTER 18

Friends Who Don't Expect You to Be Perfect

Those who wait for perfect weather will never plant seeds; those who look at every cloud will never harvest crops. Plant early in the morning, and work until evening, because you don't know if this or that will succeed. They might both do well.

Ecclesiastes 11:4,6 NCV

You live in a world where expectations are high, incredibly high, or unreachable. The media delivers an endless stream of messages that tell you how to look, how to behave, how to eat, and how to dress. The media's expectations are impossible to meet—God's are not. God doesn't expect you to be perfect . . . and neither should you.

If you find yourself bound up by the chains of perfectionism, it's time to ask yourself who you're trying to impress, and why. If you're trying to impress other people, it's time to reconsider your priorities.

Remember this: the expectations that really matter are not society's expectations or your friends' expectations. The expectations that matter are God's expectations, pure and simple. And everything else should take a back seat.

So do your best to please God, and don't worry too much about what other people think. And, when it comes to meeting the unrealistic expectations of our crazy world, forget about trying to meet those unrealistic expectations and concentrate, instead, on living a life that's pleasing to God.

The Basics:
What You Need to Know

You don't have to be perfect to be wonderful.

What the Bible Says

Your beliefs about these things should be kept secret between you and God. People are happy if they can do what they think is right without feeling guilty.
Romans 14:22 NCV

The fear of human opinion disables; trusting in God protects you from that.
Proverbs 29:25 MSG

In thee, O Lord, do I put my trust; let me never be put into confusion.
Psalm 71:1 KJV

Big Ideas

A perfectionist resists the truth that
growing up in Christ is a process.

Susan Lenzkes

We shall never come to the perfect man
til we come to the perfect world.

Matthew Henry

The happiest people in the world are not those who
have no problems, but the people who have learned to
live with those things that are less than perfect.

James Dobson

A Prayer for Today

Dear Lord, I'm certainly not perfect,
but You love me anyway.
Thank You for Your love, and for Your Son.
Amen

CHAPTER 19

Too Much Media for You and Your Friends?

Let no one deceive himself. If anyone among you seems to be wise in this age, let him become a fool that he may become wise. For the wisdom of this world is foolishness with God. For it is written, "He catches the wise in their own craftiness."

1 Corinthians 3:18-19 NKJV

Sometimes it's hard being a Christian, especially when the world keeps pumping out messages that are contrary to your faith.

The media is working around the clock in an attempt to rearrange your priorities. The media says that your appearance is all-important, that your clothes are all-important, that your car is all-important, and that partying is all-important. But guess what? Those messages are lies. The important things in your life have little to do with parties or appearances. The all-important things in life have to do with your faith, your family, and your future. Period.

Are you willing to stand up for your faith? If so, you'll be doing yourself a king-sized favor. And consider this: When you begin to speak up for God, isn't it logical to assume that you'll also begin to know Him in a more meaningful way? Of course you will.

So do yourself a favor: forget the media hype, and pay attention to God. Stand up for Him and be counted, not just in church where it's relatively easy to be a Christian, but also outside the church, where it's significantly harder. You owe it to God . . . and you owe it to yourself.

The Basics:
What You Need to Know

You and your friends shouldn't fall prey
to the media hype.

What the Bible Says

*Do not love the world or the things in the world.
If you love the world,
the love of the Father is not in you.*
1 John 2:15 NCV

*For whatever is born of God overcomes the world.
And this is the victory that has overcome the world—
our faith.*
1 John 5:4 NKJV

*Religion that God our Father accepts as pure and
faultless is this: to look after orphans and widows in
their distress and to keep oneself from
being polluted by the world.*
James 1:27 NIV

Big Ideas

Every Christian is a contradiction to this old world.
He crosses it at every point. He goes against the grain
from beginning to end. From the day that he is born
again until the day that he goes on to be with the Lord,
he must stand against the current of a world
always going the other way.

Vance Havner

A fish would never be happy living on land, because it
was made for water. An eagle could never feel satisfied
if it wasn't allowed to fly. You will never feel completely
satisfied on earth, because you were made for more.

Rick Warren

The only ultimate disaster that can befall us,
I have come to realize, is to feel ourselves to
be home on earth.

Max Lucado

A Prayer for Today

Lord, this world is a crazy place, and I have many
opportunities to stray from Your commandments.
Help me learn to obey You! Let me keep Christ in my
heart, and let me put the devil in his place:
far away from me!
Amen

CHAPTER 20

The Right Kind of Example for Your Friends

In every way be an example of doing good deeds.
When you teach, do it with honesty and seriousness.

Titus 2:7 NCV

How do people know that you're a Christian? Well, you can tell them, of course. And make no mistake about it: talking about your faith in God is a very good thing to do. But simply telling people about Jesus isn't enough. You must also be willing to show people how an extremely devoted Christian (like you) should behave.

Is your life a picture book of your creed? Do your actions line up with your beliefs? Are you willing to practice the philosophy that you preach? If so, congratulations. If not, it's time for a change.

Like it or not, your behavior is a powerful example to others. The question is not whether you will be an example to your family and friends; the question is what kind of example will you be.

Corrie ten Boom advised, "Don't worry about what you do not understand. Worry about what you do understand in the Bible but do not live by." And that's sound advice because your family and friends are always watching . . . and so, for that matter, is God.

The Basics:
What You Need to Know

You should set the right kind of example
for your friends . . . and vice-versa.

What the Bible Says

*In everything you do, stay away from complaining
and arguing, so that no one can speak a word of
blame against you. You are to live clean, innocent lives
as children of God in a dark world full of crooked
and perverse people. Let your lives shine
brightly before them.*

Philippians 2:14-15 NLT

*You are the light that gives light to the world . . . .
In the same way, you should be a light for other people.
Live so that they will see the good things you do
and will praise your Father in heaven.*

Matthew 5:14,16 NCV

*Do you want to be counted wise, to build a reputation
for wisdom? Here's what you do: Live well,
live wisely, live humbly. It's the way you live,
not the way you talk, that counts.*

James 3:13 MSG

Big Ideas

If we have the true love of God in our hearts,
we will show it in our lives. We will not have to go up
and down the earth proclaiming it.
We will show it in everything we say or do.

D. L. Moody

Among the most joyful people I have known
have been some who seem to have had no human
reason for joy. The sweet fragrance of Christ
has shown through their lives.

Elisabeth Elliot

We urgently need people who encourage and
inspire us to move toward God and away from
the world's enticing pleasures.

Jim Cymbala

A Prayer for Today

Lord, make me a worthy example to my family and
friends. And, let my words and my actions show people
how my life has been changed by You. I will praise You,
Father, by following in the footsteps of Your Son.
Let others see Him through me.
Amen

CHAPTER 21

Friends Who Encourage Your Spiritual Growth

For this reason we also, since the day we heard it, do not cease to pray for you, and to ask that you may be filled with the knowledge of His will in all wisdom and spiritual understanding.

Colossians 1:9 NKJV

When will you be a "fully-grown" Christian? Hopefully never—or at least not until you arrive in heaven! As a believer living here on planet earth, you're never "fully grown"; you always have the potential to keep growing.

Would you like a time-tested formula for spiritual growth? Here it is: keep studying God's Word, keep obeying His commandments, keep praying (and listening for answers), and keep trying to live in the center of God's will. And while you're at it, find friends who encourage you to grow. When you do these things, you'll never stay stuck for long. You will, instead, be a growing Christian . . . and that's precisely the kind of Christian God wants you to be.

The Basics:
What You Need to Know

When it comes to your faith,
there's always room for growth.

What the Bible Says

*So let us stop going over the basics of Christianity
again and again. Let us go on instead
and become mature in our understanding.*
Hebrews 6:1 NLT

*Run away from infantile indulgence. Run after mature
righteousness—faith, love, peace—joining those
who are in honest and serious prayer before God.*
2 Timothy 2:22 MSG

*For You, O God, have tested us; You have refined us
as silver is refined. You brought us into the net;
You laid affliction on our backs. You have caused men
to ride over our heads; we went through fire
and through water; but You brought
us out to rich fulfillment.*
Psalm 66:10-12 NKJV

Big Ideas

God will open up places of service for you as
He sees you are ready. Meanwhile, study the Bible
and give yourself a chance to grow.

Warren Wiersbe

Growing up in Christ is surely the most difficult,
courageous, exhilarating, and eternally
important work any of us will ever do.

Susan Lenzkes

There is nothing more important than understanding
God's truth and being changed by it, so why are we so
casual about accepting the popular theology of
the moment without checking it out for ourselves?
God has given us a mind so that we can learn and
grow. As his people, we have a great responsibility
and wonderful privilege of growing in
our understanding of him.

Sheila Walsh

A Prayer for Today

Dear Lord, the Bible tells me that You are at work in
my life, continuing to help me grow and to mature in
my faith. Show me Your wisdom, Father,
and let me live according to Your Word
and Your will.
Amen

CHAPTER 22

Your Own Worst Critic?

A devout life does bring wealth,
but it's the rich simplicity of being yourself before God.
1 Timothy 6:6 MSG

When you feel better about yourself, you'll make better choices. But sometimes, it's hard to feel good about yourself, especially when you live in a society that keeps sending out the message that you've got to be perfect.

Are you your own worst critic? And in response to that criticism, are you constantly trying to transform yourself into a person who meets society's expectations, but not God's expectations? If so, it's time to become a little more understanding of the person you see whenever you look into the mirror.

Millions of words have been written about various ways to improve self-esteem. Yet, maintaining a healthy self-image is, to a surprising extent, a matter of doing three things:

1. Obeying God
2. Thinking healthy thoughts
3. Finding things to do that please your Creator and yourself.

When you concentrate on these things, your self-image will tend to take care of itself.

The Basics:
What You Need to Know

Don't be overly critical of your friends or yourself.

What the Bible Says

You're blessed when you're content with just who you are—no more, no less. That's the moment you find yourselves proud owners of everything that can't be bought.
Matthew 5:5 MSG

God began doing a good work in you, and I am sure he will continue it until it is finished when Jesus Christ comes again.
Philippians 1:6 NCV

You made all the delicate, inner parts of my body and knit me together in my mother's womb. Thank you for making me so wonderfully complex! Your workmanship is marvelous—and how well I know it.
Psalm 139:13-14 NLT

Big Ideas

I can promise you that until you learn that solitude
is your friend and not your enemy, until you are
comfortable "staying in your own orbit,"
you will have little to give anyone else.

Luci Swindoll

Give yourself a gift today: be present with yourself.
God is. Enjoy your own personality. God does.

Barbara Johnson

It is not enough to love ourselves;
we must also like ourselves.

Joyce Meyer

A Prayer for Today

Lord, I have so much to learn and so many ways to
improve myself, but You love me just as I am.
Thank You for Your love and for Your Son.
And, help me to become the person that
You want me to become.
Amen

CHAPTER 23

The Right Kind of Dates

Are there those among you who are truly wise and understanding? Then they should show it by living right and doing good things with a gentleness that comes from wisdom.

James 3:13 NCV

s God a part of your dating life? Hopefully so. If you sincerely want to know God, then you should date people who feel the same way.

If you're still searching for Mr. or Mrs. Right (while trying to avoid falling in love with Mr. or Mrs. Wrong), be patient, be prudent, and be picky. Look for someone whose values you respect, whose behavior you approve of, and whose faith you admire. Remember that appearances can be deceiving and tempting, so watch your step. And when it comes to the important task of building a lifetime relationship with the guy or girl of your dreams, pray about it!

If you happen to be one of those very lucky ones who has already fallen madly in love with the same wonderful person who has (praise the Lord!) already fallen madly in love with you, say a great big thanks to the Matchmaker in heaven. But if you haven't yet found a soul-mate who honors both you and God, don't fret. Just keep trusting your Father in heaven, and keep yourself open to the direction in which He is leading you. And remember: When it comes to your dating life, God wants to give His approval—or not—but He won't give it until He's asked. So ask, listen, and decide accordingly.

The Basics:
What You Need to Know

When it comes to the people you date, choose wisely.

What the Bible Says

*Be sober! Be on the alert! Your adversary
the Devil is prowling around like a roaring lion,
looking for anyone he can devour.*
1 Peter 5:8 HCSB

*Light shines on the godly, and joy on those who do
right. May all who are godly be happy in
the LORD and praise his holy name.*
Psalm 97:11-12 NLT

*Blessed are the pure in heart,
because they will see God.*
Matthew 5:8 HCSB

Big Ideas

We discover our role in life through
our relationships with others.

Rick Warren

With resolve that you are going to make a relationship
work, you can develop peace treaties of love
and tolerance and harmony to transform
a difficult situation into something beautiful.

Max Lucado

Line by line, moment by moment, special times are
etched into our memories in the permanent ink of
everlasting love in our relationships.

Gloria Gaither

A Prayer for Today

Lord, I will let You rule over every aspect of my life,
including my relationships. And I know that when I do,
You will help me make choices that are right for me,
today and every day that I live.

Amen

CHAPTER 24

Friends Who Forgive

*Be even-tempered, content with second place, quick to
forgive an offense. Forgive as quickly and completely as
the Master forgave you. And regardless of
what else you put on, wear love. It's your basic,
all-purpose garment. Never be without it.*

Colossians 3:13-14 MSG

Are you the kind of person who has a tough time forgiving and forgetting? If so, welcome to the club. Most of us find it difficult to forgive the people who have hurt us. And that's too bad because life would be much simpler if we could forgive people "once and for all" and be done with it. Yet forgiveness is seldom that easy. Usually, the decision to forgive is straightforward, but the process of forgiving is more difficult. Forgiveness is a journey that requires effort, time, perseverance, and prayer.

If there exists even one person whom you have not forgiven (and that includes yourself), obey God's commandment: forgive that person today. And remember that bitterness, anger, and regret are not part of God's plan for your life. Forgiveness is.

If you sincerely wish to forgive someone, pray for that person. And then pray for yourself by asking God to heal your heart. Don't expect forgiveness to be easy or quick, but rest assured: with God as your partner, you can forgive . . . and you will.

The Basics:
What You Need to Know

It's simple: friends forgive friends.

What the Bible Says

Hatred stirs up trouble, but love forgives all wrongs.
Proverbs 10:12 NCV

Our Father is kind; you be kind. "Don't pick on people,
jump on their failures, criticize their faults—unless,
of course, you want the same treatment. Don't condemn
those who are down; that hardness can boomerang.
Be easy on people; you'll find life a lot easier."
Luke 6:36-37 MSG

Be gentle with one another, sensitive.
Forgive one another as quickly and thoroughly
as God in Christ forgave you.
Ephesians 4:32 MSG

Big Ideas

Forgiveness is the key that unlocks the door of
resentment and the handcuffs of hate.
It is a power that breaks the chains of bitterness
and the shackles of selfishness.

Corrie ten Boom

I firmly believe a great many prayers are not answered
because we are not willing to forgive someone.

D. L. Moody

Forgiveness is rarely easy, but it is always right.

Cynthia Heald

A Prayer for Today

Lord, just as You have forgiven me, I am going to forgive others. When I forgive others, I not only obey Your commandments, but I also free myself from bitterness and regret. Forgiveness is Your way, Lord, and I will make it my way, too.

Amen

CHAPTER 25

Keeping Up Appearances

And why worry about your clothes?
Look at the lilies and how they grow. They don't work
or make their clothing, yet Solomon in all his glory
was not dressed as beautifully as they are.
Matthew 6:28-29 NLT

he world sees you as you appear to be; God sees you as you really are. He sees your heart, and He understands your intentions. The opinions of others should be relatively unimportant to you; however, God's view of you—His understanding of your actions, your thoughts, and your motivations—should be vitally important.

Few things in life are more futile than "keeping up appearances" in order to impress your friends and your dates—yet the media would have you believe otherwise. The media would have you believe that everything depends on the color of your hair, the condition of your wardrobe, and the model of the car you drive. But nothing could be further from the truth. What is important, of course, is pleasing your Father in heaven. You please Him when your intentions are pure and your actions are just. When you do, you will be blessed today, tomorrow, and forever.

The Basics:
What You Need to Know

You and your friends shouldn't be
too hung up on appearances.

What the Bible Says

God does not see the same way people see.
People look at the outside of a person,
but the Lord looks at the heart.
1 Samuel 16:7 NCV

If you decide for God, living a life of God-worship,
it follows that you don't fuss about what's on the table
at mealtimes or whether the clothes in your closet are in
fashion. There is far more to your life than the food you
put in your stomach, more to your outer appearance
than the clothes you hang on your body.
Matthew 6:25 MSG

We justify our actions by appearances;
God examines our motives.
Proverbs 21:2 MSG

Big Ideas

Fashion is an enduring testimony to the fact that
we live quite consciously before the eyes of others.

John Eldredge

Outside appearances, things like the clothes you wear
or the car you drive, are important to other people
but totally unimportant to God. Trust God.

Marie T. Freeman

The life of a good religious person ought to abound
in every virtue so that he is, on the interior,
what to others he appears to be.

Thomas à Kempis

A Prayer for Today

Lord, You know my heart, and You're concerned
with the "inner me." Today, I will worry less
about what other people think . . .
and I'll worry more about what You think.
Amen

SERVICE

CHAPTER 26

Friends Who Encourage You to Serve

*So prepare your minds for service and have self-control.
All your hope should be for the gift of grace that will be
yours when Jesus Christ is shown to you.*

1 Peter 1:13 NCV

he words of Jesus are clear: the most esteemed men and women in this world are not the big-shots who jump up on stage and hog the spotlight; the greatest among us are those who are willing to become humble servants.

Are you willing to become a servant for Christ? Are you willing to pitch in and make the world a better place, or are you determined to keep all your blessings to yourself? And here's one more question: Are you willing to choose friends who encourage you to serve (by their words and by their examples)? Hopefully so.

If you seek to walk with the One from Galilee, you must become an unselfish servant. You should serve your friends quietly and without fanfare. You should find a need and fill it . . . humbly. You should lend a helping hand . . . anonymously. And you should share a word of kindness . . . with quiet sincerity.

So, as you go about your daily activities, remember this: the Savior of all humanity made Himself a servant . . . and if you want to really know Him better, you must do the same.

The Basics:
What You Need to Know

If you're a Christian, then you should also be
a servant . . . it's as simple as that.

What the Bible Says

There are different kinds of gifts, but they are all from the same Spirit. There are different ways to serve but the same Lord to serve.
1 Corinthians 12:4-5 NCV

Therefore, since we receive a kingdom which cannot be shaken, let us show gratitude, by which we may offer to God an acceptable service with reverence and awe . . . .
Hebrews 12:28 NASB

If they serve Him obediently, they will end their days in prosperity and their years in happiness.
Job 36:11 HCSB

Big Ideas

Through our service to others,
God wants to influence our world for Him.

Vonette Bright

We'll know how to lovingly serve others as
we trust him to give us the guidance we need.

Sheila Cragg

God does not do anything with us,
only through us.

Oswald Chambers

A Prayer for Today

Dear Lord, let me help others in every way that I can.
Jesus served others; I can too. I will serve other people
with my good deeds and with my prayers.
And I will give thanks for everybody who helps me.
Amen

CHAPTER 27

Friends Who Encourage You to Be a Disciplined Person

Do you not know that those who run in a race all run, but only one receives the prize? Run in such a way that you may win. Everyone who competes in the games exercises self-control in all things.

1 Corinthians 9:24-25 NASB

A re you a self-disciplined person? If so, congratulations . . . your disciplined approach to life can help you build a more meaningful relationship with God. Why? Because God expects all His believers (including you) to lead lives of disciplined obedience to Him . . . and He rewards those believers who do.

God doesn't reward laziness, misbehavior, or apathy. God is less concerned with your party time than He is with your prayer time. And God wants all His followers (including you) to behave with dignity and self-control.

Sometimes, it's hard to be dignified and disciplined. Why? Because you live in a world where many prominent people want you to believe that dignified, self-disciplined behavior is going out of style. But don't kid yourself: self-discipline never goes out of style.

Face facts: Life's greatest rewards aren't likely to fall into your lap. To the contrary, your greatest accomplishments will probably require plenty of work and a heaping helping of self-discipline—which, by the way, is perfectly fine with God. After all, He knows that you're up to the task, and He has big plans for you. God will do His part to fulfill those plans, and the rest, of course, depends upon you.

The Basics:
What You Need to Know

If you choose disciplined friends, you're more likely
to become a more disciplined person.

What the Bible Says

*I discipline my body and bring it under strict control,
so that after preaching to others,
I myself will not be disqualified.*
1 Corinthians 9:27 HCSB

*So prepare your minds for service
and have self-control.*
1 Peter 1:13 NCV

Discipline yourself for the purpose of godliness.
1 Timothy 4:7 NASB

Big Ideas

Discipline is training that develops and corrects.

Charles Stanley

Simply stated, self-discipline is obedience to
God's Word and willingness to submit everything
in life to His will, for His ultimate glory.

John MacArthur

He who obeys not the rudder will obey the reef.

Herve of Brittany

A Prayer for Today

Dear Lord, I want to be a disciplined believer.
Let me use my time wisely, let me obey Your
commandments faithfully, and let me worship
You joyfully, today and every day.
Amen

CHAPTER 28

Friends Who Help You Make Wise Choices

I am offering you life or death, blessings or curses.
Now, choose life! . . . To choose life is to love the Lord
your God, obey him, and stay close to him.

Deuteronomy 30:19-20 NCV

ace facts: your life is a series of choices. From the instant you wake up in the morning until the moment you nod off to sleep at night, you make countless decisions—decisions about the things you do, decisions about the words you speak, and decisions about the way that you choose to direct your thoughts.

As a believer who has been transformed by the radical love of Jesus, you have every reason to make wise choices. But sometimes, when the daily grind threatens to grind you up and spit you out, you may make choices that are displeasing to God. When you do, you'll pay a price because you'll forfeit the happiness and the peace that might otherwise have been yours.

So, as you pause to consider the kind of Christian you are—and the kind of Christian you want to become—ask yourself whether you're sitting on the fence or standing in the light. And while you're at it, ask yourself whether you're choosing friends who help you make smart choices, not dumb ones. Remember: if you sincerely want to follow in the footsteps of the One from Galilee, you must make choices that are pleasing to Him. He deserves no less . . . and neither, for that matter, do you.

The Basics:
What You Need to Know

Make friends with people who will help you
make wise choices.

What the Bible Says

*The thing you should want most is God's kingdom
and doing what God wants. Then all these other things
you need will be given to you.*

Matthew 6:33 NCV

*Now it happened as they went that He entered
a certain village; and a certain woman named Martha
welcomed Him into her house. And she had a sister
called Mary, who also sat at Jesus' feet and heard His
word. But Martha was distracted with much serving,
and she approached Him and said, "Lord, do You not
care that my sister has left me to serve alone? Therefore
tell her to help me." And Jesus answered and said to
her, "Martha, Martha, you are worried and troubled
about many things. But one thing is needed,
and Mary has chosen that good part,
which will not be taken away from her."*

Luke 10:38-42 NKJV

Big Ideas

Every day of our lives we make choices about
how we're going to live that day.

Luci Swindoll

We are either the masters or the victims of our attitudes.
It is a matter of personal choice. Who we are today is
the result of choices we made yesterday.
Tomorrow, we will become what we choose today.
To change means to choose to change.

John Maxwell

To refuse to respond is in itself a response.

Madeleine L'Engle

A Prayer for Today

Lord, help me to make choices that are pleasing to You.
Help me to be honest, patient, and kind.
And above all, help me to follow the teachings of Jesus,
not just today, but every day.
Amen

CHAPTER 29

Friends Who Encourage You to Praise the Creator

Is anyone happy? Let him sing songs of praise.
James 5:13 NIV

f you're like most folks on the planet, you're a very busy person. Your life is probably hectic, demanding, and complicated. And when the demands of life leave you rushing from place to place with scarcely a moment to spare, you may not take time to praise your Creator. Big mistake.

The Bible makes it clear: it pays to praise God. Worship and praise should be a part of everything you do. Otherwise, you quickly lose perspective as you fall prey to the demands of everyday life.

Do you and your friends sincerely desire to know God in a more meaningful way? Then praise Him for who He is and for what He has done for you. And please don't wait until Sunday morning—praise Him all day long, every day, for as long as you live . . . and then for all eternity.

The Basics:
What You Need to Know

You and your friends should praise God.

What the Bible Says

*Through Him then, let us continually offer up
a sacrifice of praise to God, that is,
the fruit of lips that give thanks to His name.*
Hebrews 13:15 NASB

*The LORD is my strength and song, and He has become
my salvation; He is my God, and I will praise Him.*
Exodus 15:2 NIV

*And suddenly there was with the angel a multitude of
the heavenly host praising God and saying:
"Glory to God in the highest, And on earth peace,
goodwill toward men!"*
Luke 2:13-14 NKJV

Big Ideas

I am to praise God for all things, regardless of
where they seem to originate. Doing this is the key to
receiving the blessings of God.
Praise will wash away my resentments.

Catherine Marshall

The time for universal praise is sure to come some day.
Let us begin to do our part now.

Hannah Whitall Smith

Praise is a means of taking back territory from the devil.

Joey Johnson

A Prayer for Today

Heavenly Father, today and every day I will praise You.
I will praise You with my thoughts, my prayers,
my words, and my deeds . . . now and forever.
Amen

CHAPTER 30

Friends Who Follow Christ

Be imitators of God, therefore,
as dearly loved children.

Ephesians 5:1 NIV

hom will you walk with today? Will you and your friends walk with people who worship the ways of the world? Or will you walk with the Son of God?

Jesus walks with you. Are you walking with Him? Hopefully, you will choose to walk with Him today and every day of your life.

Jesus has called upon believers of every generation (and that includes you) to follow in His footsteps. And God's Word promises that when you follow in Christ's footsteps, you will learn how to live freely and lightly (Matthew 11:28-30).

Are you worried about the day ahead? Be confident in God's power. He will never desert you. Are you concerned about the future? Be courageous and call upon God. He will protect you. Are you confused? Listen to the quiet voice of your Heavenly Father. He is not a God of confusion. Talk with God; listen to Him; follow His commandments . . . and walk with His Son—starting now.

The Basics:
What You Need to Know

It's up to you to follow Christ,
and one good way to do it is to find friends
who will follow Him with you.

What the Bible Says

Work hard, but not just to please your masters when they are watching. As slaves of Christ, do the will of God with all your heart. Work with enthusiasm, as though you were working for the Lord rather than for people.

Ephesians 6:6-7 NLT

Then Jesus said to His disciples,
"If anyone wants to come with Me, he must deny himself, take up his cross, and follow Me."

Matthew 16:24 HCSB

All of us who look forward to his Coming stay ready, with the glistening purity of Jesus' life as a model for our own.

1 John 3:3 MSG

Big Ideas

How often it occurs to me, as it must to you,
that it is far easier simply to cooperate with God!

Beth Moore

As we seek to become disciples of Jesus Christ,
we should never forget that the word disciple is directly
related to the word discipline. To be a disciple of
the Lord Jesus Christ is to know his discipline.

Dennis Swanberg

You cannot cooperate with Jesus in becoming what He
wants you to become and simultaneously be what the
world desires to make you. If you would say, "Take the
world but give me Jesus," then you must deny yourself
and take up your cross. The simple truth is that your
"self" must be put to death in order for you to get to
the point where for you to live is Christ. What will it be?
The world and you, or Jesus and you?
You do have a choice to make.

Kay Arthur

A Prayer for Today

Dear Lord, thank You for the gift of Your Son Jesus,
my personal Savior. Let me be a worthy disciple of
Christ, and let me be ever grateful for His love. I offer
my life to You, Lord, so that I might live according to
Your commandments and according to Your plan.
I will praise You always as I give thanks for Your Son
and for Your everlasting love.

Amen

Bible Verses
to Memorize

Finally brothers, whatever is true, whatever is honorable, whatever is just, whatever is pure, whatever is lovely, whatever is commendable—if there is any moral excellence and if there is any praise—dwell on these things.

Philippians 4:8 HCSB

All Scripture is inspired by God and is profitable
for teaching, for rebuking, for correcting,
for training in righteousness,
so that the man of God may be complete,
equipped for every good work.

2 Timothy 3:16-17 HCSB

This is the day the LORD has made. We will rejoice and be glad in it.

Psalm 118:24 NLT

Therefore, brothers, by the mercies of God,
I urge you to present your bodies as
a living sacrifice, holy and pleasing to God;
this is your spiritual worship.

Romans 12:1 HCSB

For to me to live is Christ, and to die is gain.

Philippians 1:21 KJV

Be kind to each other,
tenderhearted, forgiving
one another, just as God through
Christ has forgiven you.

Ephesians 4:32 NLT

But God demonstrates His own love toward us, in that while we were still sinners, Christ died for us.

Romans 5:8 NKJV

A good name is to be chosen over great wealth.

Proverbs 22:1 HCSB

For where two or three come together in my name, there am I with them.

Matthew 18:20 NIV

A joyful heart makes a face cheerful.

Proverbs 15:13 HCSB

And I am convinced that nothing
can ever separate us from his love.
Whether we are high above the sky
or in the deepest ocean, nothing
in all creation will ever be able to
separate us from the love of God that
is revealed in Christ Jesus our Lord.

Romans 8:38-39 NLT

If we confess our sins,
He is faithful and righteous
to forgive us our sins
and to cleanse us from
all unrighteousness.

1 John 1:9 HCSB

*I have learned,
in whatsoever state I am,
therewith to be content.*

Philippians 4:11 KJV

WE MUST OBEY GOD RATHER THAN MEN.

Acts 5:29 HCSB

Therefore, if anyone
is in Christ,
he is a new creation;
the old has gone,
the new has come!

2 Corinthians 5:17 NIV

**Keep your lives free from
the love of money and be content with
what you have, because God has said,
"Never will I leave you;
never will I forsake you."**

Hebrews 13:5 NIV

For God so loved
the world that He gave
His only begotten Son,
that whoever believes
in Him should not perish
but have everlasting life.

John 3:16 NKJV